Creating HTML5 Animations with Flash and Wallaby

Ian McLean

Beijing · Cambridge · Farnham · Köln · Sebastopol · Tokyo

Adobe Developer Library, a copublishing partnership between O'Reilly Media Inc., and Adobe Systems, Inc., is the authoritative resource for developers using Adobe technologies. These comprehensive resources offer learning solutions to help developers create cutting-edge interactive web applications that can reach virtually anyone on any platform.

With top-quality books and innovative online resources covering the latest tools for rich-Internet application development, the *Adobe Developer Library* delivers expert training straight from the source. Topics include ActionScript, Adobe Flex®, Adobe Flash®, and Adobe Acrobat®.

Get the latest news about books, online resources, and more at *http://adobedeveloper library.com*.

Creating HTML5 Animations with Flash and Wallaby

by Ian McLean

Published by O'Reilly Media, Inc., 1005 Gravenstein Highway North, Sebastopol, CA 95472.

O'Reilly books may be purchased for educational, business, or sales promotional use. Online editions are also available for most titles (*http://my.safaribooksonline.com*). For more information, contact our corporate/institutional sales department: (800) 998-9938 or *corporate@oreilly.com*.

Editor: Mary Treseler		**Cover Designer:** Karen Montgomery	
Production Editor: Jasmine Perez		**Interior Designer:** David Futato	
Copyeditor: Audrey Doyle		**Illustrator:** Robert Romano	
Proofreader: O'Reilly Production Services			

ISBN: 978-1-449-30713-4

[LSI]

1314904119

My sincerest thanks goes out to my love, Jana, for graciously tolerating the number of times I asked her "does this sound right?" and to my family for penny pinching to buy me my first PowerPC computer so many years ago.

Table of Contents

Preface

What Is Wallaby?

Adobe Wallaby is a tool that is used to convert animated content created in Flash Professional to HTML5 so that it may be viewed using many of the standards-compliant browsers available today. In doing so, Wallaby enables you to use a mature animation tool, like Flash Professional, to produce compelling animations and creative content for the standard Web.

Put simply, Wallaby means that creating standards-compliant animations for the Web just got *a lot* easier for everybody.

You'll also be happy to know that all iOS-based devices are fair game as well. That means it is open season in terms of creating Flash content that can be displayed on the iPhone and iPad.

Until now, the big challenge in creating HTML5 animations was that you had to be a skilled JavaScript developer to pull it off. Assuming you were said developer, the amount of effort involved in creating HTML5 animations programmatically was still far too time-consuming, as it required writing code to draw your shapes, code to load any potential bitmap assets, and code for all the necessary translations of those items over time. Also, considering there was no built-in mechanism to manage the chronology of your animations, such as a timeline provides, to time your animations you had to monitor the count of a timer.

Creating HTML5 animations also proved challenging for designers, as it required them to write code. While there are some great "devsigners" out there who know both design and development, having to get involved with code to build an animation isn't exactly most designers' cup of tea.

There is a greater issue at hand here, though: designers and developers are often cut from different cloth. A developer probably shouldn't be given creative control of any animation unless you want to see some very interesting results. At the same time, a designer might struggle with writing code when charged with having to create animations programmatically. When you consider this, you realize how the state of creating animations on the standard Web has been completely backward; it has forced developers to act as designers and designers to act as developers.

The good news is that if you're a creative type, Wallaby puts you right back in the game of creating animations for the standard Web. If you're a developer, provided you can learn some Flash Professional basics, you can spend just 30 minutes creating an animation rather than several hours. These are really big wins for designers and developers alike.

A Brief History of Flash and HTML5

These days, some people view Flash and HTML5 as competing technologies, even though a good number of the capabilities of these technologies are starting to converge. It's true that HTML5 has improved substantially over HTML4 and seeks to offer a lot of the same features of Flash. Whether one of these technologies will fully replace the other is unknown; it seems far more likely that they will simply continue to coexist. Regardless, there is no denying the fact that Flash has provided a means of creating complex animation and interactivity on the Web for many years. However, HTML has offered a standard and universally accessible format for representing data on the Web that is openly visible to search engines. Because of this, Flash and HTML have often been used in complementary ways; you will find numerous examples of sites leveraging HTML as a foundation to display data and Flash to achieve a more sophisticated level of animation or interactivity.

Concerns in Reaching Audiences

Although the number of people with Flash Player is significantly high, a portion of those users still don't have Flash. Therefore, it's safe to presume that if you're targeting Flash users, some people will turn away because they won't make an effort to install the Flash plug-in or because their device simply doesn't support it. On the other hand, HTML5 works out of the box in modern browsers, and therefore, projects that seek to reach the largest audience possible tend to rely solely on HTML5 to power their content. In some cases, this can mean sacrificing some of the capabilities of Flash and, more specifically, some of things that were easier to do in Flash, such as creating animations, and designing a site with a lesser level of animation and interactivity.

The idea behind Wallaby is to give you some of the best of both worlds: use Flash to easily create engaging animations while maintaining the widest reach in terms of audience by targeting HTML5.

I would be remiss if I didn't mention that HTML5 doesn't solve every challenge in reaching our audience. Although the HTML5 specification is a standard supported by most modern browsers, many people still continue to use older browsers. For example, much to the dismay of many web developers, a significant number of people still use

Internet Explorer 6, especially in the corporate realm. If your project must be viewable by browsers new and old, you might choose to avoid the features of HTML5 entirely and stick with HTML4. Although the number of people using older browsers will continue to decrease with time, gaps in your reachable audience will always exist. Just make sure to consider this when deciding on a technology for your project, and you'll be fine.

Now, assuming you've already considered this and HTML5 is your weapon of choice, great; Wallaby will put you on the fast track to creating HTML5 experiences with engaging animations.

Browser Support

Wallaby in its current form makes heavy use of WebKit-specific CCS3 tags. This means that non-WebKit-based browsers such as Firefox and IE9 will not fully support Wallaby-generated animations.

However, browsers like Chrome, Safari, and Mobile Safari are fair game.

Conversion Limitations

While the ability to use a visual tool such as Flash Professional to create HTML5 simplifies the process of creating animations, it's important to recognize that Wallaby can't be perfect at crafting the most optimized code possible. For highly complex animations where optimal performance is critical, it's often best to get "closer to the metal" and work directly with JavaScript and HTML rather than using a visual tool to create this code for you.

Another limitation is that Wallaby really only supports those features of Flash that are relevant to creating an animation. For instance, it won't have much success in converting your complex AS3 game to HTML5. However, it does support all the features necessary to streamline the creation of animations.

Who This Book Is For

This book is intended for anyone who wants to create HTML5-based animations using Flash Professional and wants to skip the additional work of coding these animations by hand. You might be a designer who is looking for a means to generate HTML5 content, or you might be a developer who is looking for a faster way to create animations than the fully programmatic approach provides. Either way, to benefit from this book you won't need any previous experience with Flash Professional.

A note about scope: Flash Professional is covered in this book, but being that our focus is on creating HTML5, we will stick to the material relevant to that process. The content within is fairly comprehensive and will help you to become familiar with the application as well as give you the skills necessary to create many different types of animations using Flash Professional. Even so, Flash Professional has many advanced techniques and tips beyond what is covered in this book. If you want to learn even more about Flash Professional, there are many great books out there for those who want to obtain rock-star-like skills.

Content Approach

This book covers everything you need to know to create HTML5 animations, whether you are a novice or an expert Flash user. Chapter 1 and Chapter 2 focus on providing those who are new to Flash with a background on the tool, its features, and concepts regarding its use. Chapter 3 through Chapter 5 focus on the Wallaby-specific aspects of using Flash, its supported features, caveats, and the process of making your content live.

With this in mind, those who are comfortable with creating content in Flash may wish to focus on Chapter 3 through Chapter 5. If you're new to Flash, feel free to simply take it from the top.

System Requirements

If you plan to use Flash Professional to create HTML5 animations, you'll need Flash Professional CS5 or later. Also, as with any application, your system needs to meet certain requirements in order to run the software. Adobe suggests the following, as a minimum:

Windows

- Intel Pentium 4 or AMD Athlon 64 processor
- 3.5 GB of available hard-disk space for installation; additional free space required during installation (cannot install on removable Flash storage devices)
- 1024 × 768 display (1280 × 800 recommended) with 16-bit video card
- DVD-ROM drive
- QuickTime 7.6.2 software required for multimedia features
- Broadband Internet connection required for online services

Mac OS

- Multicore Intel processor
- Mac OS X v10.5.8 or v10.6
- 1 GB of RAM (2 GB recommended)
- 4 GB of available hard-disk space for installation; additional free space required during installation (cannot install on a volume that uses a case-sensitive file system or on removable Flash storage devices)

- 1024 × 768 display (1280 × 800 recommended) with 16-bit video card
- DVD-ROM drive
- QuickTime 7.6.2 software required for multimedia features
- Broadband Internet connection required for online services

Conventions Used in This Book

The following typographical conventions are used in this book:

Italic

> Indicates new terms, URLs, email addresses, filenames, and file extensions.

`Constant width`

> Used for program listings, as well as within paragraphs to refer to program elements such as variable or function names, databases, data types, environment variables, statements, and keywords.

`Constant width bold`

> Shows commands or other text that should be typed literally by the user.

`Constant width italic`

> Shows text that should be replaced with user-supplied values or by values determined by context.

 This icon signifies a tip, suggestion, or general note.

 This icon indicates a warning or caution.

Using Code Examples

This book is here to help you get your job done. In general, you may use the code in this book in your programs and documentation. You do not need to contact us for permission unless you're reproducing a significant portion of the code. For example, writing a program that uses several chunks of code from this book does not require permission. Selling or distributing a CD-ROM of examples from O'Reilly books does require permission. Answering a question by citing this book and quoting example code does not require permission. Incorporating a significant amount of example code from this book into your product's documentation does require permission.

We appreciate, but do not require, attribution. An attribution usually includes the title, author, publisher, and ISBN. For example: "*Creating HTML5 Animations with Flash and Wallaby* by Ian McLean (O'Reilly). Copyright 2011 Ian McLean, 978-1-449-30713-4."

If you feel your use of code examples falls outside fair use or the permission given above, feel free to contact us at *permissions@oreilly.com*.

Safari® Books Online

Safari Books Online is an on-demand digital library that lets you easily search over 7,500 technology and creative reference books and videos to find the answers you need quickly.

With a subscription, you can read any page and watch any video from our library online. Read books on your cell phone and mobile devices. Access new titles before they are available for print, and get exclusive access to manuscripts in development and post feedback for the authors. Copy and paste code samples, organize your favorites, download chapters, bookmark key sections, create notes, print out pages, and benefit from tons of other time-saving features.

O'Reilly Media has uploaded this book to the Safari Books Online service. To have full digital access to this book and others on similar topics from O'Reilly and other publishers, sign up for free at *http://my.safaribooksonline.com*.

How to Contact Us

Please address comments and questions concerning this book to the publisher:

O'Reilly Media, Inc.
1005 Gravenstein Highway North
Sebastopol, CA 95472
800-998-9938 (in the United States or Canada)
707-829-0515 (international or local)
707-829-0104 (fax)

We have a web page for this book, where we list errata, examples, and any additional information. You can access this page at:

http://www.oreilly.com/catalog/9781449307134

To comment or ask technical questions about this book, send email to:

bookquestions@oreilly.com

For more information about our books, courses, conferences, and news, see our website at *http://www.oreilly.com*.

Find us on Facebook: *http://facebook.com/oreilly*

Follow us on Twitter: *http://twitter.com/oreillymedia*

Watch us on YouTube: *http://www.youtube.com/oreillymedia*

CHAPTER 1

Flash Professional Basics

Flash Professional is a popular tool used to author a wide variety of creative and interactive content that can be deployed to the Web and mobile devices. It can even be used to create desktop applications. There are many aspects to the application itself, but its most notable characteristic is a timeline and asset-centric interface that makes it ideal for creating animations. Until recently, Flash-created content was only viewable by devices with support for Flash.

Now, when combined with Wallaby, Flash Professional can be used to create HTML5-based animations as well.

At this point, you might be wondering why we would bother using an application intended to create Flash content to instead create HTML5 animations. After all, aren't we talking apples and elephants here? The answer is both yes and no. Sure, Flash and HTML5 are different technologies with different implementations for powering content on the Web. However, if we look at creating animations from an artistic perspective, the workflow is really one and the same. Flash Professional provides an advanced visual interface to create animated content that really accelerates this workflow. This remains true regardless of whether that content is ultimately powered by Flash or by HTML5. In fact, Flash Professional is one of the first tools, if not *the* first tool, on the market that allows you to take a visual approach to creating HTML5 animations versus a fully programmatic approach.

As an animation tool, Flash Professional is well seasoned. The first incantation of the Flash software actually debuted in 1996 as an application called FutureSplash Animator. It was then given the name Flash after being purchased by Macromedia not long after its release. At the time, the visual capabilities of Flash went far beyond the capabilities of HTML; that led to widespread use of Flash on the Web. Today Flash Professional is part of the Adobe Creative Suite of products and has evolved into a very powerful and feature-rich tool responsible for much of the content on the Web.

Before we go any further, it bears mentioning that Flash Professional is just one tool within the family of the Flash Platform. In fact, because of the versatility of Flash Player itself, there are several tools, each of which takes a different approach to creating content. The common thread among these tools is that they all produce content that is powered by the *Flash Player runtime*. There is, however, one new exception to this, in that Flash Professional animation projects can now be exported to HTML5. This means that animations created with Flash can run on the standard Web without the need for a plug-in.

The Flash Platform

For the purposes of creating HTML5 animations, we will focus almost entirely on Flash Professional and the Adobe Wallaby export tool. However, creating HTML5 animations is just one capability of Flash Professional. That being said, having a basic understanding of the playing field in terms of Flash tools and technologies can help you feel more at home as you explore the Flash Professional user interface. It will also help you better understand what pertains to the HTML5 workflow and what doesn't.

Let's have a look at a few of the terms and technologies you'll encounter as you build your animation:

Flash Professional
> As I mentioned, Flash Professional is a timeline-based tool for creating animations and interactive experiences that we'll be working with to author our HTML5 content.
>
> As of the writing of this book, the current version is Flash Professional CS5.

FLA files
> FLA files are Flash Professional project files. These are the files that Wallaby requires when converting your content.
>
> FLA files have an extension of *.fla*.

Flash Player
> Flash Player is the runtime that typically executes all Flash content. Of course, the animations we export to HTML5 are the exception to this. Flash Player often comes in the form of a browser plug-in but can be standalone as well.
>
> As of the writing of this book, the current major version is Flash Player 10.

SWF files
> SWF files are the output files that are published from Flash Professional and can be played with Flash Player. Since our output will be HTML5 markup, we won't be exporting a SWF when we're done. We will, however, be publishing SWFs during the creation of our animations in order to preview them before we take the final step of exporting them to HTML5.
>
> SWF files have an extension of *.swf*.

ActionScript

ActionScript is Flash's scripting language. Although AS3 has a very broad set of capabilities, you won't need to learn much more than a few lines. Our usage of AS3 will be more or less limited to handling buttons clicks and basic frame navigation. Anything beyond that isn't relevant when creating our animations, and thus isn't supported by the Wallaby Exporter.

As of the writing of this book, the current version is ActionScript 3.

Now that you have an understanding of the platform and its moving parts, Flash Professional should make a bit more sense to you. Keep in mind that the Flash Platform features many other tools beyond what I've covered here. You won't need any knowledge of these as far as HTML5 animations are concerned, but feel free to explore them all the same.

Flash Professional at a Glance

Now that we've covered the fundamentals of the Flash Platform, let's dive into the Flash Professional application.

As I mentioned before, you'll be spending the majority of your time with Flash Professional. From here on out, when I refer to "Flash" I will be speaking strictly of Flash Professional. This will help to eliminate any confusion between the terms *Flash* and *Flash Player* or *Flash Platform* as we move forward.

The Flash user interface has several different panels and windows for performing various tasks, but from a 1,000-foot view it is really composed of three main parts (see Figure 1-1):

- The *Library* which is used to store assets
- The *Stage* which is like a drawing canvas for assets
- The *Timeline* which is used to build animations

As you create your animation, you will, for the most part, be creating assets in the Library, placing them on the Stage, and then using the Timeline to animate them. (Although that was a fairly simplistic statement, it does a good job of describing the general workflow in Flash.)

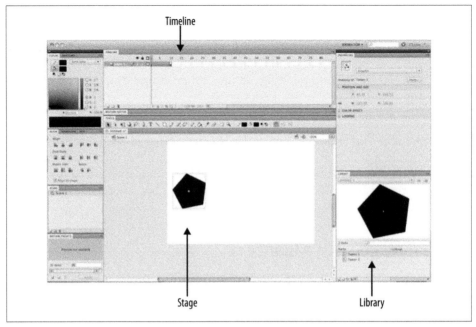

Figure 1-1. The Flash Professional CS5 interface

The Library

The Library in Flash is simply an area that stores all the various parts of your animation in one place. Items in the Library can be renamed, deleted, or organized into folders as needed. These items can be images, video, audio, or items called *symbols*. We'll discuss symbols in more detail in just a second, but first, let's look at how you'll arrange these items in your animation.

The Stage

If you've worked with graphics programs in the past, the Stage is probably a very familiar concept. The Stage is the content area where your animation lives visually. Items can be placed anywhere on the Stage, or even off-stage. Items off-stage aren't visible to those viewing the animation. For example, you might use off-stage items to create an effect of an item flying onto the screen from the outside.

By accessing the Modify→Document Settings menu, you can configure the Stage in terms of its dimensions and its background color to suit the needs of your animation. You can also change the units on the Stage to whatever you're most comfortable with. Figure 1-2 shows the settings you can configure in the Document Settings window.

Keep in mind that when your animation is ultimately viewed in a browser, its dimensions can be different from what you set here. This is because additional size and scaling information may be specified within the HTML page. As such, an animation could potentially change its size and scaling options.

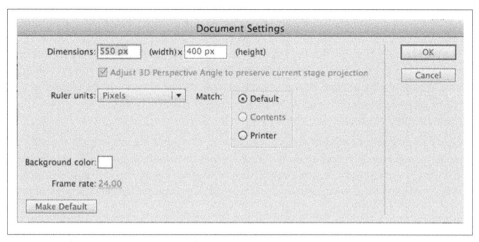

Figure 1-2. The Document Settings window

Lastly, from this window, you can change the frame rate for the animation, which brings us to our next topic.

The Timeline

The concept behind the Timeline in Flash Professional is a lot like a reel of film played on a projector. The Timeline, as shown in Figure 1-3, contains a series of movie-like cells, known as *frames*, which can be displayed back-to-back in order to create motion. The speed at which these frames are played is known as the *frame rate* or *frames per second* (which is often abbreviated to *fps*).

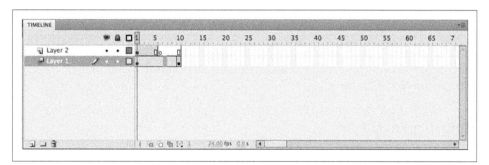

Figure 1-3. The Timeline

The frame rate inevitably affects how the animation appears to the eye. The lower the animation's frame rate, the more the animation looks like a slide show. Conversely, the higher the animation's frame rate, the more fluid the animation appears. The default frame rate for a Flash project is 24 fps, which also happens to be the standard frame rate of film. This will usually suffice for most animations. Alternatively, some users may prefer 30 fps, the standard frame rate of NTSC, as it provides some additional fluidity. If your animation requires highly fluid movement, you can set your frame rate as high as you need to; keep in mind, though, that the highest value isn't always the best. High frame rates can tax the CPU and result in faulty playback. Also note that if you change your animation's frame rate in the middle of your project, you will be changing the speed of all your animated parts as well. This is why it's best to decide on a frame rate at the start of your project.

Similar to a program like Photoshop or Illustrator, the Timeline also supports *layers* as a means of separating visual elements into distinct levels (see Figure 1-4). Layers can be extremely useful when creating animations with many parts by giving you a means of organization. You also can move layers up and down to change their display depth.

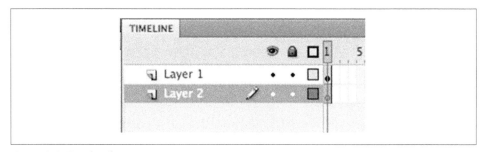

Figure 1-4. Timeline layers

When you're viewing the Stage with multiple layers you're actually seeing the result of all these layers being stacked one on top of the other. However, if you were to hide all the layers and focus on a single layer, you would see that the content of that layer is, in fact, separated from the rest.

Ultimately, the Timeline, with the help of what are called *keyframes*, is what you'll use to design the movement of your animations through a process called *tweening*. We'll come back to keyframes and tweening later; first let's have a closer look at how we work with assets in Flash.

Importing Assets

Provided the file you're trying to import is supported, you can use the File→Import menu option to easily import your assets into Flash.

By default, Flash supports major media types and formats for images, video, and audio. While the application itself supports these types, we must stay mindful of what is supported by the HTML5 exporter, and more importantly, what isn't. Specifically, Wallaby doesn't support video and audio media types. As such, when creating animations you'll probably want to limit your imports to images or vector graphics created in a program like Illustrator. Doing so will help to ensure that your animations export properly when you're finished.

Drawing Shapes

Flash Professional has a toolbar similar to what you might find in Photoshop or Illustrator. From this Tools pane (see Figure 1-5), you can create shapes or text as well as manipulate their position and scale on the Stage.

Figure 1-5. The Tools pane

Anything you draw in Flash takes the form of a *shape*. Shapes in Flash are vector graphics that are drawn at display time from a stored algorithm. The algorithm is essentially a blueprint; it fully describes all aspects of the shape. Figure 1-6 shows a shape with editable vertices.

Figure 1-6. A shape with editable vertices

A major benefit of using vector graphics in a project is that they can be scaled and manipulated to any size or shape without losing quality. Shapes are also very malleable;

you can change their shape at any time. You can even use tweens to morph between two different shapes, which we'll cover in a bit.

Working with Images

When you want to use an existing picture or you need something that doesn't make sense to draw in Flash, you will typically import an image. When importing an image into Flash, regardless of its format or compression, it becomes a *bitmap*.

Bitmaps, as opposed to graphics, are bitmapped images such as JPEGs or PNGs. Bitmaps contain per-pixel data used to describe the image rather than an algorithm. Since there is no formulaic representation of a bitmap, when a bitmap is scaled it loses image clarity, as shown in Figure 1-7. This effect is far more dramatic when scaling bitmaps above their original size because the necessary image data simply doesn't exist; it must be intelligently guessed based on the existing pixel data. Creating data that doesn't exist is far more difficult than throwing away data that does exist; hence scaling bitmaps down tends to generate good results. Regardless, scaling too far in either direction proves to be problematic at some point.

Figure 1-7. A bitmap which has become lossy because it has been scaled too high

Knowing When to Use Bitmaps or Shapes

If bitmaps have so many constraints, you might wonder why we don't simply rely on vector graphics entirely. The answer is that complex vector graphics come at a high performance cost. For example, you would want to refrain from converting a highly detailed photo of a person's face into a vector graphic. The complexity of the formula needed to represent the image as a vector graphic would not only be far greater than a bitmap of the same image, but would also cause considerable strain on your CPU. In turn, this would likely cause choppy playback when viewing the animation.

Deciding when to use bitmaps or shapes depends on what you need to accomplish. If you need higher detail, using a bitmap makes sense. If you need an asset that you can change or morph, graphics are a better alternative.

If you need a mixture of both, you can actually convert an image to a graphic, although you will probably need to play around with it to see if you can maintain an acceptable level of detail without winding up with a vector representation that is too complex.

Avoiding Undesired Scaling in Bitmaps

There is also another important thing to consider when using bitmaps. As I mentioned, bitmaps can lose quality when they are scaled. With that in mind, it's important to consider how your animation will scale when viewed at different resolutions or on different devices, and the effect it will have on the bitmaps in the animation.

Sometimes the animation isn't scaled at all; you set a fixed width and height for the content and it's viewed at that size regardless of the device being used. In this case, you can use bitmaps to your heart's content and no loss of quality will occur since there is no scaling involved.

If you aren't working with a fixed width, you've probably set your content to scale so as to take up as much of the screen as possible. In this case, you have to be more careful. For example, say you have an animation with a document size of 1024 × 768 that has a background image that is also 1024 × 768. The animation has been placed within a page so that it expands to the maximum size possible. If someone using an iPad views the image, there is almost no loss in quality. This is because the screen resolution of the iPad is 1024 × 768 and little to no scaling needs to occur to fill the screen. Now, if the same animation is viewed on a monitor with a higher resolution of 1920 × 1080, the animation will scale considerably to take up the full screen and a very noticeable loss of quality will occur in the background image. In a case like this, it might have made more sense to design the animation using a shape as the background so that it would maintain its quality.

As you can see, there are several considerations to keep in mind when building your animations. And there are many more beyond what I can reasonably cover here. Sometimes the best solution can only result from simple trial and error. Even so, if you put the effort into thinking through your approach before building an animation, you're bound to save yourself a lot of time.

Converting Assets to Symbols

Once you've imported or drawn something on the Stage in Flash, the next step is typically to convert it into a *symbol*. A symbol is simply a container for content that makes it reusable within the animation by allowing you to create *instances*. We'll cover instances and their benefits in just a moment, but for now, let's look at the different forms a symbol can take.

When you create a symbol you have the option of specifying the behavior of a movie clip, graphic, or button (see Figure 1-8).

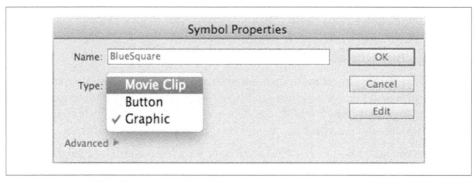

Figure 1-8. A symbol with a set type of Graphic

The movie clip is the most commonly used symbol in Flash. A movie clip is simply a timeline-based symbol that acts as a container for animations so that they don't always have to live directly on the main Timeline of your document. A key thing to remember about a movie clip is that it has an independent timeline. This means its playback isn't linked to the playback of the main Timeline in any way. A movie clip also allows frame navigation actions and interactivity using ActionScript.

A graphic is very similar to a movie clip with the exception that it does *not* have an independent timeline. The playback of a graphic is directly tied to the playback of the main Timeline. Additionally, a graphic doesn't support any interactivity via Action-Script.

Buttons are more or less what they sound like. When creating a symbol with the behavior of a button, you'll have a frame for each state of the button's interaction; up, down, and over (see Figure 1-9). Button symbols allow you to easily build buttons with custom visual states.

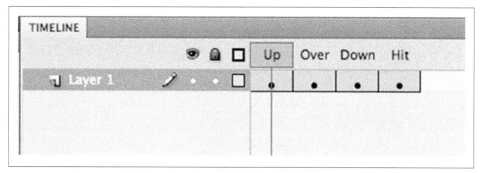

Figure 1-9. A button symbol

The type of symbol you choose to create depends on what you're trying to achieve. Graphics are best suited for static assets and individual pieces of an animation. Movie clips are often ideal for constructing animations using those pieces. Buttons are used to capture user input so that you can do things like stop or replay the animation or provide a means of navigating to a specific point on the Timeline.

Instances

Any symbol in the Library that is placed on the Stage creates what is called an *instance* of that asset. An instance, in this case, just means that Flash uses the same description in the Library to draw the asset on the Stage, regardless of how many of those assets are actually placed. The end result of this is that you can place an item on the Stage 100 times without increasing the size needed store to the animation on disk.

Since speed is essential when viewing content on the Web, this sort of small footprint becomes very desirable. This, however, doesn't mean there is no cost to having several instances of the same asset on the screen at once. In this case, more system resources, like CPU and memory, are required in order for the asset to be drawn; and this is as true for HTML5 as it is for anything else.

In terms of performance, modern-day desktop and laptop computers are so fast that they rarely have any trouble handling the complex content we throw at them. Mobile devices, on the other hand, have only a fraction of the power of traditional computers. This means a far greater emphasis on optimizing your content is required if you intend to produce mobile content. Thankfully, you can stay out of trouble if you understand some basics about computer resources and how they'll be used. We'll discuss this optimization in greater detail in Chapter 3.

Keyframes

Keyframes are nothing more than frames that are used to define what should be visible on the Stage starting at a particular point in time.

A keyframe can be several frames in length as well. The length of a keyframe instructs Flash that its contents should continue to be displayed on-screen until the last frame is reached or until a new keyframe is encountered.

Flash also has what are known as *blank keyframes*. These indicate that nothing is to be displayed on the Stage at that time. To create a blank keyframe you can add a new keyframe to the Timeline or take an existing keyframe and delete all of its content on the Stage. Figure 1-10 shows a keyframe and a blank keyframe.

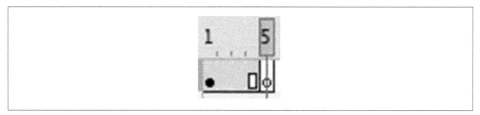

Figure 1-10. A keyframe and a blank keyframe

Once you have two keyframes on the Timeline, you can create a *tween*.

Tweening

For a cartoon animator who draws each frame by hand, a series of consecutive keyframes might do the job just fine. In fact, some animators use Flash in just this way. For the rest of us, hand-drawing frame-by-frame animations can become extremely time-consuming. To eliminate the need to draw all of the in-between parts of an animation Flash Professional offers a technique appropriately named *tweening*. Tweening allows you to design a transformation of a visual asset over a period of time and have all the necessary steps in between created for you.

A couple of different types of tweens are available in Flash. A *motion tween* can automate changes in position, rotation, scale, and skew (see Figure 1-11). It can also automate value changes for color and filter effects that are available in Flash.

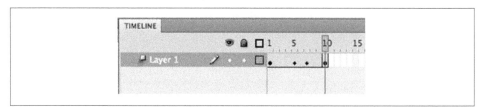

Figure 1-11. A motion tween with independent keyframes on the Timeline

Because motion tweens can get very complex, they actually contain their own keyframes that are independent of those found directly on the Timeline. These keyframes can still be edited from the main Timeline, but a far more advanced editor called the *Motion Editor* exists that provides finer control when animating (see Figure 1-12).

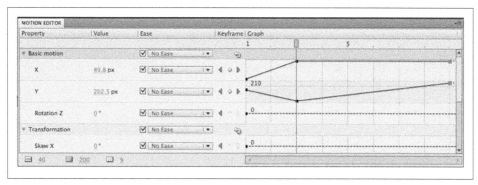

Figure 1-12. The Motion Editor

There is also another type of tween known as a *shape tween*. A shape tween is what it sounds like; it allows you to animate changes in a shape, as shown in Figure 1-13. This can be accomplished in two ways. The first method is to create two keyframes over which a single shape changes its form. The second method is to create keyframes with two completely different shapes, in which case Flash will blend or *morph* between them.

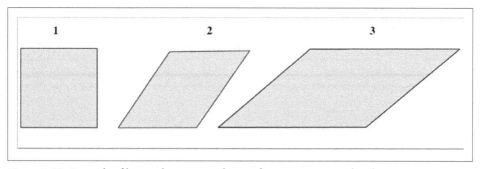

Figure 1-13. Example of how a shape tween changes from a square to a rhombus

A *classic tween* is the much simpler predecessor to a motion tween. Classic tweens work in the same way as motion tweens except that classic tweens lack their own self-contained keyframes (see Figure 1-14). Classic tweens are also incompatible with the Motion Editor. Instead, they use keyframes placed directly on the Timeline.

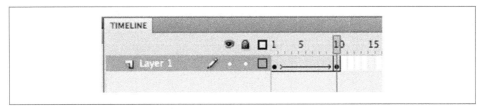

Figure 1-14. A classic tween

Now that we've had a basic overview of Flash we can move right into creating our first Wallaby animation.

CHAPTER 2

Creating a Basic HTML5 Animation

For your first animation you will build a simple scrolling text marquis. This will be very similar to the old HTML `<marquis>` tag, and while it isn't exactly fancy, it's a perfectly simple example to start with.

Once you're done, you'll need the Adobe Wallaby application to export the animation. If you haven't installed it already, take a moment to download it from the Adobe Labs website (*http://labs.adobe.com/*).

Creating a New Project

Before you begin building your animation, you'll need to create a new project in Flash. Select File→New to access the New Document window (see Figure 2-1).

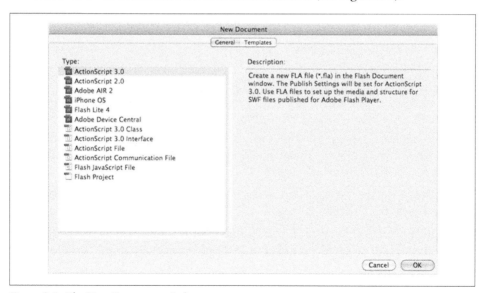

Figure 2-1. The New Document window

Here you'll see several different options for creating a new document. For our purposes, we want to create an ActionScript 3.0 document, so select ActionScript 3.0 and click OK.

Flash will open a new project where you'll be presented with a blank canvas where you will draw and animate your text.

Creating the Text

At this point, you're ready to create your text, so go to the toolbar and select the Text tool (**T**), as shown in Figure 2-2).

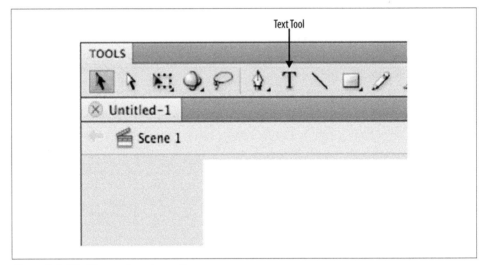

Figure 2-2. The Text tool on the toolbar

With the Text tool selected, go ahead and click anywhere on the Stage to get a text cursor, and then write a message out of which you want to create a marquis (see Figure 2-3).

Now that you have some text on the Stage you are ready to animate it. As I mentioned in Chapter 1, if you want to animate an item on the Stage, the first step is to convert the item to a symbol in your Library.

To do so just select the text you've created and then use the Modify→Convert to Symbol option, or press the F8 key.

Once you've created your symbol, you'll notice that it's now an item in your Library that you can use to create any number of additional instances on the Stage (see Figure 2-4).

Note that there's no need to drag this to the Stage since your already existing text is now an instance of this as well.

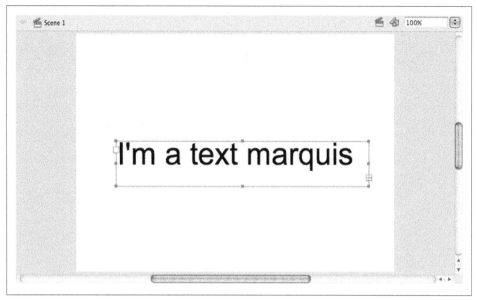

Figure 2-3. Text creation with the Text tool

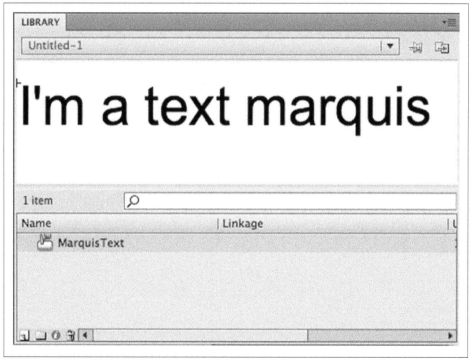

Figure 2-4. A symbol in the Library

Animating the Marquis

With your marquis symbol on the Stage you can now animate it. To achieve the scrolling effect you need a keyframe where you'll position the text outside the visible Stage so that you can animate it scrolling by.

Looking at the Timeline you'll notice that a keyframe was already created for you when you created your text item on the Stage (see Figure 2-5).

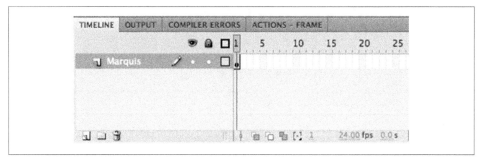

Figure 2-5. The keyframe containing the text item

To position the text item outside the visible Stage, just select it and drag it to the right until you're past the Stage boundaries (see Figure 2-6).

Figure 2-6. The text item moved to the right, outside the visible content area

Now that that's off the screen you want to animate it across the screen to the left to give a scrolling effect. Click on a later frame on the Timeline (say, frame 20), right-click, and select the Insert Keyframe option from the context menu. Notice that this creates a keyframe with identical content to the earlier keyframe on the Timeline (see Figure 2-7).

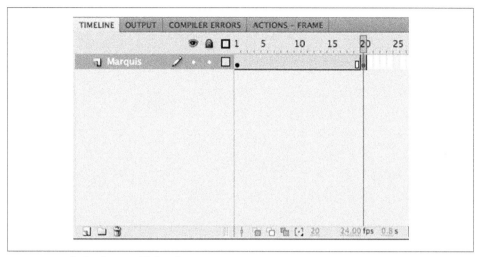

Figure 2-7. The keyframe added at frame 20

Next, with the new keyframe selected, grab the text item on the Stage and drag it back to the left until it is outside the visible Stage area (see Figure 2-8). To make sure there is no y-axis movement you can hold down the Shift key while you drag.

Figure 2-8. The text item moved to the left, outside the visible content area

Now that you've created the necessary keyframes and positioned the start and end points of your text animation all that is left to do is to create the tween. Click anywhere between the two keyframes and right-click to create a classic tween (see Figure 2-9).

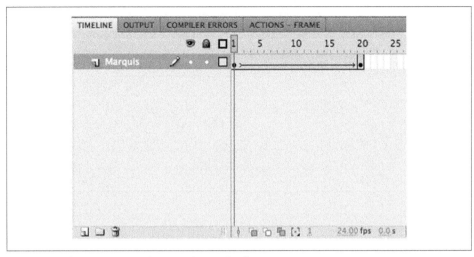

Figure 2-9. The motion tween between the two keyframes

With your tween created you can publish the document to view the resultant animation (see Figure 2-10). Do so by selecting the Control→Test Movie→Test option, or simply use the Shift-Return key shortcut.

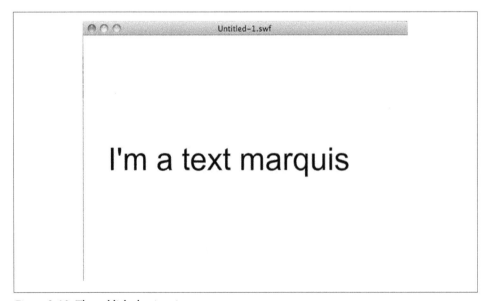

Figure 2-10. The published animation

At this point, you should see your marquis continuously scrolling from left to right. Notice that the animation does not stop at the last frame but continues to loop. This is because looping is the default behavior of a movie clip in Flash.

Go ahead and close the animation; then use the File→Save menu option to name the file (e.g., *marqui.fla*), and save your project somewhere on your hard disk. Remember this location because you'll be loading this file into Wallaby in just a moment.

Exporting the HTML5 Animation from Wallaby

Once you've opened Wallaby, there are only a couple of steps to export your animation. First click the Browse button and select the Flash project file (*.fla* file) that you saved just a moment ago (see Figure 2-11).

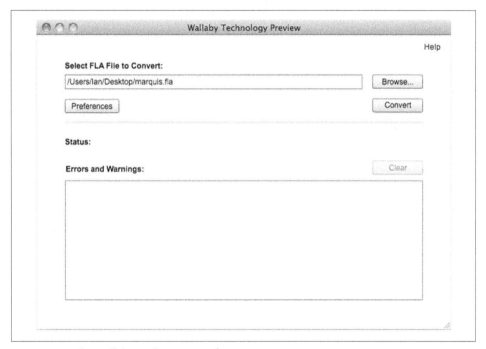

Figure 2-11. The Wallaby application interface

With the *.fla* file selected go ahead and click the Convert button. You'll be asked to name your HTML file. Give it the name "marquis.html" and click Save to start the conversion. You'll see a message in the Status area when the conversion process is complete.

At this point, your animation is ready to be viewed. If you navigate to the folder where you exported your HTML, you'll see the *marquis.html* file along with some other supporting files (see Figure 2-12). These files are required to drive the animation, so make sure they remain in the same directory.

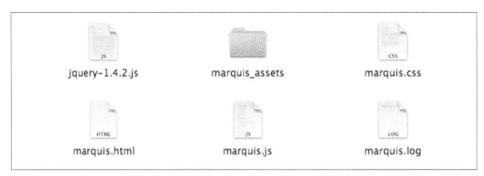

Figure 2-12. The Wallaby exported files

If you double-click on *marquis.html*, your animation will load in your default browser. Now you can sit back and enjoy the fruits of your labor: an HTML5 marquis animation that can be viewed on any standards-compliant browser and a multitude of devices.

With a basic animation under our belt, we'll move on to Chapter 3 and cover some tips pertaining to the creation of more complex animations.

Creating Advanced Animations

When building animations it's important that you don't introduce things into your animations that don't export. The last thing you want to do is to spend several hours tweaking an animation that previews in Flash, only to discover that Wallaby doesn't support some aspect of it.

As I mentioned before, Wallaby can't possibly support all of the many features of Flash. Here is a list of what it *does* support, along with some usage tips:

Timeline

Wallaby supports the Flash Timeline, keyframes, and tweens. Support for nested timelines (movie clips) does exist, although it's suggested that animations should be designed primarily on Flash's main Timeline where possible.

Layers

Standard layers, guide layers, and mask layers are supported within animations.

Wallaby only supports masks with a duration that lasts the duration of the frame. If you make a partial mask on a layer, it will generate an error. Masks, when converted, can also put significant strain on less powerful devices. As such, be careful when using complicated masking, and be sure to keep the number of masks in your animation at a minimum.

ActionScript

Wallaby provides no support for any ActionScript, with one exception: the stop() command. Putting stop() on the final frame of an animation allows you to specify that the animation should not loop. Otherwise, all animations will loop by default.

Symbols

Symbols and symbol identifiers are supported in Wallaby. In fact, symbol identifiers are carried through to resultant HTML5 code, making it much easier to implement interactivity to individual parts of your animation using JavaScript after the fact. We'll touch on this in the "Adding Basic Interactivity" section of Chapter 5.

Filters

Alpha filters are the only filters currently supported by Wallaby.

Shapes

In general, any vector graphics you can create in Flash can be converted in Wallaby. This includes all shape tools, and the pen and pencil tools.

Strokes

Wallaby supports strokes of any size. Stroke styles, on the other hand, are limited to hairline, solid, and dashed.

Fills

Wallaby supports gradient-based fills, image-based fills, and solid colors.

Images

Wallaby supports any images that can be imported into Flash. Image transparency is also supported, but this will depend largely on the transparency support in the browser where the animation is being viewed.

Buttons

Buttons with normal, hover, and active states can be designed using Flash and exported with Wallaby. When exported and viewed in a browser these buttons will change their states per the user's interaction. However, since there is no ActionScript support within Wallaby, any button-click actions, such as navigating to a new page, will need to be added after the export using JavaScript.

Paths

Motion paths can be used in order to animate your visual assets along a path.

Text

Wallaby provides support for standard text and some TLF text. When using TLF text, make sure you do a few text exports early on to ensure that your text content is supported.

Tweens

Wallaby supports classic tweens, motion tweens, and shape tweens.

Build your animation with these supported features, and come conversion time, you should have few issues. After you've exported, the next step will be to ensure that the animation performs well in the browser.

Building for Performance

Before you start creating that complex animation that is going to blow everyone away, it's important to understand a bit about performance tuning. As with any project, working fast and seeing fast results can be exciting, but if you aren't diligent in organizing your project and trimming the fat as you add complexity, the performance of the final product will really suffer.

In our case, there is a reason why performance tuning is especially important. If you've ever worked with visual tools for creating web content or visual tools that export any kind of programmatic code, you may have noticed that the tools fail to be telepathic. By this I mean that while these tools do their best to translate what you do into code, they can't know exactly how you intend to use any of the code, and therefore the code they generate can be somewhat generic and/or poorly structured. Effectively, this means the generated code, although functional, rarely performs as well as something that was handwritten and optimized for the task. Wallaby isn't exempt from this rule, and while it will work fine for the creation of most animations, those of you who are making exceptionally complicated animations may encounter some poor performance from Wallaby that you wouldn't experience if the same animation were generated by some handwritten JavaScript optimized for the task. It's likely that performance won't be an issue for most of the animations you will export, but if you're attempting something complicated there are some things to keep in mind to ensure that your resultant animation can perform as well as possible.

When we use Wallaby we're really asking one technology (Flash) to create content for a completely different technology (HTML5). With this kind of approach there are challenges due to the large delta between how those technologies handle things.

Consequently, not everything that runs well in Flash Player runs well in a browser.

I'm not simply referring to unsupported features of Flash that cannot be translated to HTML5, but rather to the performance of your successfully exported animation. That being said, when building more complicated animations you'll want to pay close attention to optimizing your project so that the final product will run smoothly.

Here are a few guidelines to accomplish this.

Export and Test Often

I can't stress how important this is if you're attempting a more complicated animation. You want to avoid the situation where you've spent several days building an animation, only to discover at the 11th hour that it doesn't run well in a browser. At that stage of the game, you'll have a very difficult time determining the point at which things became too complicated or what you should do to attempt to fix the performance issues.

If instead you export frequently after making significant changes, you'll be less likely to waste days building a bad animation and you'll be able to identify and resolve issues before it's too late.

Take the Right Approach

Let's imagine that you want to make an animation with falling snow and you want each snowflake to have some variation.

One approach could be to make 50 different snowflakes, each as a highly detailed transparent image. You could then import them, scale them each to a different size, and animate them individually so that they fall and rotate at the same time.

While this might create a realistic-looking snowfall effect, it does so in a way that creates a lot of strain on the browser. Each snowflake has to be held separately in memory, and then each one must be translated during each step of the animation.

Another approach that could accomplish something very similar is to create one large image with snowflakes of different designs, sizes, and rotations, and simply animate it so that it moves downward, thus creating the illusion of falling snow. This approach requires much less effort on behalf of the browser and would allow you to create several additional animated elements in your animation before reaching its performance limitations.

Stay Mindful of Bandwidth

If you've developed anything for the Web in the past, you know the value of maintaining a low kilobyte weight to ensure fast load times. Wallaby exports your assets in the same form that you include them in your project and makes no effort to appropriately size or compress them beyond what you have prepared. Make sure you apply the same care and consideration to preparing and handling the assets for animation as you would for anything else. For example, you would want to avoid including needlessly large or uncompressed images if the way in which you are using those images doesn't necessitate such a high quality.

Determine the Limitations

Naturally the browsers and devices that your audience is using aren't all created equally.

Here's an example. Safari, unlike Chrome, supports GPU acceleration, giving it some advantage in rendering some more complex animations on devices equipped with a powerful GPU such as an iPad or iPhone. On the other hand, the optimizations of the V8 JavaScript engine within Chrome coupled with the more powerful CPUs found in desktops and newer tablets offer some advantage as well.

The trick, however, is not to determine the browser and device combination that will run your animation the fastest, but rather to determine the slowest browser and device combination that you wish to support. You'll need to draw a line as to the minimum hardware and browsers that you expect to support, and this is how you can determine how complicated your animation can be and how much effort you'll need to put into tuning its performance.

If, on the other hand, you only intend to target a specific device and browser combination, you're free to create animations that leverage the full potential of each.

Wallaby-Specific Performance Tips

There are a few features that run great in Flash but, when converted to HTML5, require a lot of JavaScript code to pull off. As a rule, the more complex the generated code, the more the browser has to work, which can result in poor animation performance. With that being said, here are just a few Wallaby-specific performance tips to help you create lightweight and well-performing animations:

Use motion tweens
> In Wallaby, motion tweens can be converted to HTML5 in a far more efficient fashion than frame-by-frame animations. Avoid using the latter altogether if possible, and focus on using tweens to create animations.

Minimize shape tweens
> Shape tweens, although supported, can result in a lot of generated JavaScript and can place some strain on the browser. Use them sparingly in order to ensure that your animation performs well.

Use simple paths
> Motion paths are typically OK, but try to avoid using exceptionally complex paths as they can have a negative effect on performance.

Now that we've greatly raised the chances of building a supported and well-performing animation for conversion, let's take a closer look at the Wallaby interface and the process of conversion.

CHAPTER 4

Using Wallaby

Before getting started, remember that your document file must be produced with Flash Professional CS5 or later in order for it to work.

If you haven't downloaded Wallaby yet, do so now. You can download an installer for either Mac OS or Windows from the Adobe Labs website (*http://labs.adobe.com/tech nologies/wallaby/*); once you've downloaded the installer, run it.

Converting Animations

Now, in order to convert your animation, open Wallaby and click the Browse button to locate your Flash document. Once you've selected it, go ahead and click Convert (see Figure 4-1).

Wallaby will ask you where you want to save the resultant *.html* file. This is slightly misleading because Wallaby will actually be exporting the *.html* file and all the additional files necessary to power your animation. As such, it makes sense to create a new folder for your animation. This saves you from having to hunt down each of Wallaby's files in a cluttered folder.

Once the export is complete, you can open your folder and you should see something similar to Figure 4-2.

We'll cover how to actually use these files in your site in the next chapter, but for now, let's look at the individual files:

jquery-1.4.2.js
    JQuery is a JavaScript library that's used for creating the different aspects of the animation. This is always included in the main *.html* file.

marquis_assets
    This folder contains the individual assets needed for the animation, in SVG format.

marquis.css
    This file contains all the CSS information for the animation.

marquis.html

> This is the animation's main *.html* file containing the necessary HTML markup for the animation.

marquis.js

> All of the generated JavaScript code that performs the animation is in this file.

marquis.log

> This is a logfile containing information about the export process.

Each of these files is necessary to power the animation. Be sure to keep them within the same folder. If you decide to move them around, that's fine; just make sure you update the file references in the *.html* file to reflect the changes, or the animation won't work.

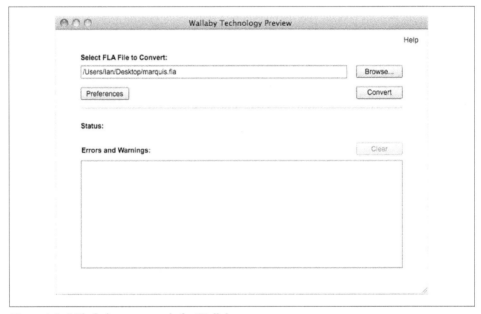

Figure 4-1. A Flash document ready for Wallaby to convert

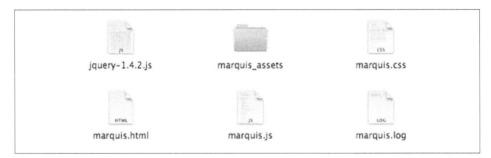

Figure 4-2. The resultant files exported for the animation

Preferences

If you click the Preferences button in Wallaby, you'll get a couple of options—specifically, Preview in Default Browser and Enable Logging (see Figure 4-3).

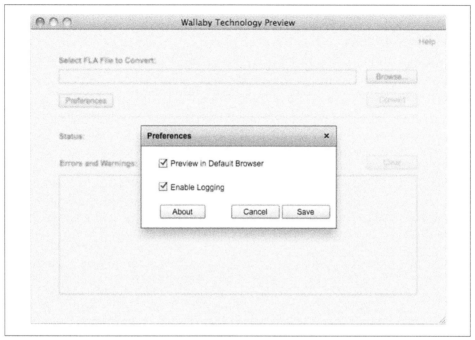

Figure 4-3. Wallaby Preferences

Both of these options are fairly self-explanatory. If you deselect Preview in Default Browser, your animation will not automatically open after the conversion is complete. Enable Logging, if selected, will generate a logfile in the export directory containing information about the export process. This can be useful for taking a close look at a project that may be generating a lot of errors. If no errors exist, this logfile will simply log the details of your successful export (see Figure 4-4).

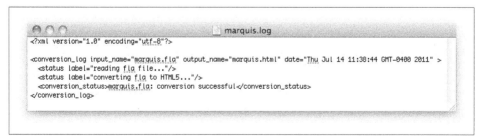

Figure 4-4. A successful export log

Status

During the export process, the Status area will basically tell you when the conversion is in process and when it has finished. If there were errors in the project, the Status area will reflect this; otherwise, it will show a success message.

Errors and Warnings

All errors and warnings during the export process are echoed to the Errors and Warnings text area. When you are developing your animation this area is critical in terms of telling you whether you've used an unsupported feature in your animation project.

Whereas errors will prevent the project from exporting, warnings will allow the project to export. Some warnings can potentially be overlooked, but make sure you check your animation and ensure that the results are as expected. For example, if I were to try to convert a project with lines with a line style of hatched I would get a warning informing me that this specific line style is unsupported (see Figure 4-5). If this line style were critical to the design I wanted for the animation, I might want to consider creating that effect in a way that is supported by the exporter. If it didn't matter, I could just disregard this warning.

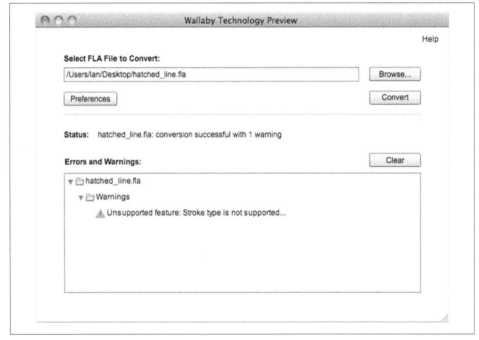

Figure 4-5. A warning about an unsupported feature

All told, the Wallaby tool is very basic and easy to use. If you've been careful to avoid any unsupported features of Flash and you've periodically kept an eye on the performance of your animation while you were building it, you should be able to export your final animation without a hitch.

Next we'll look at how to incorporate your animation into your existing content or site.

CHAPTER 5

Using Wallaby Animations

After you've exported your animation, you probably will want to incorporate it into an existing page somehow. If a JavaScript guru is available to help you, great; otherwise, you'll need to dig into the HTML and JavaScript and do a quick transplant of your animation code into your existing page.

Placing the Animation

Before we get started, keep in mind that, although your content will likely be more complex than this, the process we're about to cover will be more or less the same regardless of the content's complexity.

Now, even though the "splash" page is a widely known faux pas these days, for the sake of our basic example let's say that you want to make one anyway. With that in mind, let's assume you've created the following HTML document named *enter.html* with a link that says "Enter site":

```
enter.html
<!DOCTYPE html>
<!-- Created with Adobe(R) technology -->
<html>
  <head>
    <meta charset="utf-8"></meta>
  </head>
  <body>
    <a href="main.html">Enter Site</a>
  </body>
</html>
```

In order to finish the page, you want your animation to appear above the "Enter Site" link on this page. We'll use our scrolling marquis example from Chapter 2 as the animation to be placed.

Begin by copying the files necessary for the animation into the directory containing your existing HTML content. Let's look at the files that were exported from our scrolling marquis animation, in Figure 5-1.

Figure 5-1. Exported marquis animation

Copy the *marquis_assets*, *marquis.css*, and *marquis.js* files, as well as the *jquery-1.4.2.js* JQuery library, into the directory containing your existing HTML content.

 If your existing HTML already has the JQuery library included, there is no need to copy or include it a second time.

After you have copied the files, update the *enter.html* markup so that it includes the CSS and JavaScript necessary for your animation:

```
enter.html
<!DOCTYPE html>
<!-- Created with Adobe(R) technology -->
<html>
  <head>
    <meta charset="utf-8"></meta>
    <link href="marquis.css" type="text/css" rel="stylesheet"></link>
    <script type="text/javascript" src="jquery-1.4.2.js"></script>
    <script type="text/javascript" src="marquis.js"></script>
  </head>
  <body>
    <a href="main.html">Enter Site</a>
  </body>
</html>
```

Next, you want to grab the HTML markup that contains your animation from the exported animation source.

The source of your marquis animation looks like this:

```
marquis.html
<!DOCTYPE html>
<!-- Created with Adobe(R) technology -->
<html>
  <head>
    <meta charset="utf-8"></meta>
    <link href="marquis.css" type="text/css" rel="stylesheet"></link>
    <script type="text/javascript" src="jquery-1.4.2.js"></script>
    <script type="text/javascript" src="marquis.js"></script>
  </head>
  <body>
    <div class="wlby_movie">
      <div class="wlby_1 wlby_sprite">
        <div class="wlby_2 wlby_fs">
          <!-- Start of symbol: MarquisText -->
          <div class="wlby_button">
            <div class="wlby_button_normal wlby_button_hover wlby_button_active">
              <img src="marquis_assets/svgblock_0.svg" class="wlby_3"></img>
            </div>
          </div>
          <!-- End of symbol: MarquisText -->
        </div>
        <div class="wlby_4">
          <div class="wlby_5">
            <!-- Start of symbol: MarquisText -->
            <div class="wlby_button">
              <div class="wlby_button_normal wlby_button_hover wlby_button_active">
                <img src="marquis_assets/svgblock_1.svg" class="wlby_3"></img>
              </div>
            </div>
            <!-- End of symbol: MarquisText -->
          </div>
        </div>
      </div>
    </div>
  </body>
</html>
```

Initially this might look a little complicated, but the only thing that needs to be identified in this code is the div with the class name of wlby_movie. This is the div that contains the markup related to your animation. Go ahead and select wlby_movie and its contents, and copy it so that you can place it in your *enter.html* markup.

Now place the `wlby_movie` div and its contents into your existing page, beneath your `<body>` tag:

```
enter.html
<!DOCTYPE html>
<!-- Created with Adobe(R) technology -->
<html>
  <head>
    <meta charset="utf-8"></meta>
    <link href="marquis.css" type="text/css" rel="stylesheet"></link>
    <script type="text/javascript" src="jquery-1.4.2.js"></script>
    <script type="text/javascript" src="marquis.js"></script>
  </head>
  <body>
    <div class="wlby_movie">
      <div class="wlby_1 wlby_sprite">
        <div class="wlby_2 wlby_fs">
          <!-- Start of symbol: MarquisText -->
          <div class="wlby_button">
            <div class="wlby_button_normal wlby_button_hover wlby_button_active">
              <img src="marquis_assets/svgblock_0.svg" class="wlby_3"></img>
            </div>
          </div>
          <!-- End of symbol: MarquisText -->
        </div>
        <div class="wlby_4">
          <div class="wlby_5">
            <!-- Start of symbol: MarquisText -->
            <div class="wlby_button">
              <div class="wlby_button_normal wlby_button_hover wlby_button_active">
                <img src="marquis_assets/svgblock_1.svg" class="wlby_3"></img>
              </div>
            </div>
            <!-- End of symbol: MarquisText -->
          </div>
        </div>
      </div>
    </div>

    <a href="main.html">Enter Site</a>
  </body>
</html>
```

Now that your animation markup has been placed and all the necessary CSS and Java-Script have been included you're ready to view your animation by opening *enter.html* in a browser and viewing the results (see Figure 5-2).

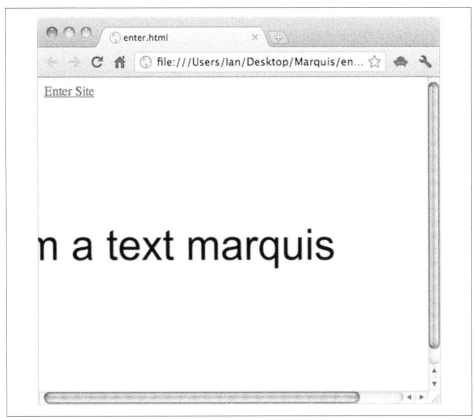

Figure 5-2. The animation running within the existing HTML

At this point, the animation should be successfully placed within your existing page. You might notice, though, that your "Enter Site" link is actually above the animation when instead you want it below. This is because when Wallaby generates the CSS for the `wlby_movie` div its CSS positioning defaults to absolute. This means the animation will calculate its positions based on the browser window rather than from within the div in which you've placed it. Therefore, you need to update the CSS in the *marquis.css* file that you included in the page so that the `wlby_movie` div positioning is relative:

```
div.wlby_movie
{
    overflow: hidden;
    position: relative;
    left: 0px;
    top: 0px;
    width: 550px;
    height: 400px;
}
```

Now your animation should determine its placement relative to its containing divider and your link will appear like you would expect (see Figure 5-3).

Figure 5-3. The animation with relative positioning

And with that, your animation has been successfully placed within your existing content, and its positioning has been updated so that it remains within your designated content area.

Adding Basic Interactivity

Because Wallaby offers no real ActionScript support, you must add interactivity to your animation at this point, after you've converted your content.

Working off our existing example, let's assume that we'd like someone viewing this page to be able to enter the site by clicking on the marquis text as well. In order to enable this capability, you can add some basic JQuery to your code, but you need an easy means of referencing the text content in the animation, either as an *ID* or as a *class*. Depending on the complexity of the animation, it can become difficult to isolate the aspect of the animation which you want to be interactive, and this is precisely why Wallaby supports *symbol identifiers*.

Going back to our Flash project, select the text instance on the Stage and open the Properties panel from the Window→Properties menu item. In the field at the top you can assign an identifier to the symbol (see Figure 5-4).

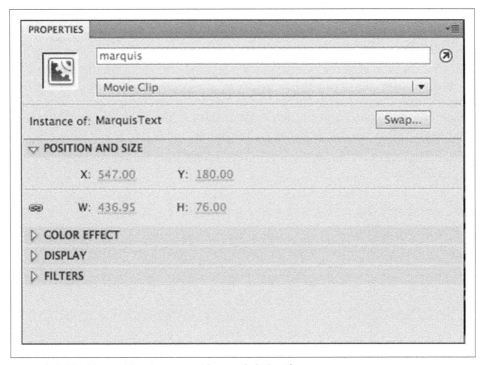

Figure 5-4. The MarquisText instance with a symbol identifier

In this case, I've used "marquis" as the symbol identifier. Had we done this before the earlier conversion process, we would have seen the following in our code:

```
<div class="wlby_movie">
    <div class="wlby_1 marquis">
      <!-- Start of symbol: MarquisText -->
      <img src="marquis_assets/svgblock_0.svg" class="wlby_2"></img>
      <!-- End of symbol: MarquisText -->
    </div>
</div>
```

Now, having set an identifier, the div containing the marquis text now has a class name of `wlby_1 marquis`. The name of the identifier has been appended to the div class.

Now that this has been done, you can easily reference the marquis text using JQuery in order to add interactivity. Open the *marquis.js* file and place the following code at the top:

```
$(document).ready(function() {
$('.marquis').click(function(){
window.location = "main.html";
});
}
```

This is a bit of JavaScript and JQuery that takes your marquis object and tells a function to fire when the marquis is clicked. The function then tells the browser to take you to the *main.html* portion of your site.

Now your user can click the animation and enter the site. Although this is what you sought to achieve, it's hardly the extent to which you can add interactivity to your animation. With a greater understanding of JavaScript and JQuery, as well as some knowledge of the generated code from your animation, there are seemingly vast possibilities as to what you can do with your animation.

Now go forth and have fun creating your own HTML5 animations and exploring all the possibilities!

About the Author

Ian McLean is a Flash platform enthusiast, speaker, and technical writer who has been building enterprise applications for over 10 years. An expert in Flex and AIR, Ian also maintains a strong interest in emerging development tools, processes, and practices. Ian has a background in game development and masquerades as a producer and mastering engineer in his free time.

Get even more for your money.

Join the O'Reilly Community, and register the O'Reilly books you own. It's free, and you'll get:

- $4.99 ebook upgrade offer
- 40% upgrade offer on O'Reilly print books
- Membership discounts on books and events
- Free lifetime updates to ebooks and videos
- Multiple ebook formats, DRM FREE
- Participation in the O'Reilly community
- Newsletters
- Account management
- 100% Satisfaction Guarantee

Signing up is easy:

1. **Go to: oreilly.com/go/register**
2. **Create an O'Reilly login.**
3. **Provide your address.**
4. **Register your books.**

Note: English-language books only

To order books online:
oreilly.com/store

For questions about products or an order:
orders@oreilly.com

To sign up to get topic-specific email announcements and/or news about upcoming books, conferences, special offers, and new technologies:
elists@oreilly.com

For technical questions about book content:
booktech@oreilly.com

To submit new book proposals to our editors:
proposals@oreilly.com

O'Reilly books are available in multiple DRM-free ebook formats. For more information:
oreilly.com/ebooks

O'REILLY®

Spreading the knowledge of innovators   oreilly.com

The information you need, when and where you need it.

With Safari Books Online, you can:

Access the contents of thousands of technology and business books

- Quickly search over 7000 books and certification guides
- Download whole books or chapters in PDF format, at no extra cost, to print or read on the go
- Copy and paste code
- Save up to 35% on O'Reilly print books
- **New!** Access mobile-friendly books directly from cell phones and mobile devices

Stay up-to-date on emerging topics before the books are published

- Get on-demand access to evolving manuscripts.
- Interact directly with authors of upcoming books

Explore thousands of hours of video on technology and design topics

- Learn from expert video tutorials
- Watch and replay recorded conference sessions

Spreading the knowledge of innovators   safari.oreilly.com